The Country Without a Post Office

ALSO BY AGHA SHAHID ALI

POETRY

Call Me Ishmael Tonight
Rooms Are Never Finished
The Belovéd Witness: Selected Poems
A Nostalgist's Map of America
A Walk Through the Yellow Pages
The Half-Inch Himalayas
In Memory of Begum Akhtar & Other Poems
Bone-Sculpture

TRANSLATION

The Rebel's Silhouette: Selected Poems (Faiz Ahmed Faiz)

CRITICISM

T. S. Eliot as Editor
Ravishing DisUnities: Real Ghazals in English (editor)

The Country Without a Post Office

Poems

AGHA SHAHID ALI

W. W. NORTON & COMPANY
NEW YORK / LONDON

Copyright © 1997 by Agha Shahid Ali
All rights reserved
Printed in the United States of America
First published as a Norton paperback 1998

For information about permission to reproduce selections from this book,
write to Permissions, W. W. Norton & Company, Inc., 500 Fifth Avenue,
New York, NY 10110.

The text of this book is composed in Weiss
with the display set in Lilith Bold
Composition by Gina Webster on desktop using QuarkXpress 3.31
Manufacturing by The Courier Companies, Inc.
Book design by Susan Hood

Library of Congress Cataloging-in-Publication Data
Agha, Shahid Ali, date.
    The country without a post office : poems / Agha Shahid Ali.
        p.   cm.
    ISBN 0-393-04057-7
    1. Jammu and Kashmir (India)—Poetry. I. Title.
PR9499.3.A39C68   1997
821—dc20   96-38242
                                                    CIP

ISBN-0-393-31761-7 pbk

W. W. Norton & Company, Inc., 500 Fifth Avenue, New York, N.Y. 10110
www.wwnorton.com

W. W. Norton & Company Ltd., Castle House, 75/76 Wells Street, London W1T 3QT

4 5 6 7 8 9 0

FOR MY MOTHER —SUFIA—

THE BRAVEST OF THEM—

& OF US—

ALL

& FOR JAMES MERRILL (1926–1995)
IN "THE RAPTURE OF REVISING"

Acknowledgments

A Fellowship from the John Simon Guggenheim Foundation and an Artist's Fellowship for Poetry from the New York Foundation for the Arts helped me greatly.

These poems—often in different form—appeared in the following places:

The Alembic: "Ghazal" ("Rumors of spring . . .")
Anseo: "The Last Saffron"
The Asian Pacific American Journal: "A Footnote to History"
Denver Quarterly: "The Correspondent" "I See Kashmir from
    New Delhi at Midnight"
Field: "The Blesséd Word" in an earlier essay version
Graham House Review: "The Country Without a Post Office"
    as "Kashmir Without a Post Office"
Grand Street: "Ghazal" ("The only language of loss . . .")
Greenfield Review: "A Footnote to History"
Harvard Review: "Some Vision of the World Cashmere"
Kenyon Review: "Farewell" "The Floating Post Office"
    "Lo, A Tint Cashmere! / Lo, A Rose!"
Massachusetts Review: "A Villanelle" "Ghazal" ("Where are
    you . . .")

The Nation: "Hans Christian Ostro"

Orion: "A Pastoral"

Painted Bride Quarterly: "Son et Lumière at Shalimar Garden"

Paris Review: "A History of Paisley" "After the August Wedding in Lahore, Pakistan,"

Poetry: "At the Museum"

Poetry Review: "The Country Without a Post Office"

The Prose Poem: An International Journal: "Dear Shahid,"

Quarterly West: "A Pastoral"

Samar: "Son et Lumière at Shalimar Garden"

Seneca Review: "The Last Saffron"

Sonora Review: "Death Row"

TriQuarterly: "A Fate's Brief Memoir" "The Blesséd Word" "The City of Daughters"

Verse: "Return to Harmony 3"

Xanadu: "At the Museum" in an earlier version

Yale Review: "Muharram in Srinagar, 1992"

"A Pastoral" was issued as a limited edition broadside by Mummy Mountain Press in 1993. Gratitude to Karla Elling's letterpress finesse.

"Muharram in Srinagar, 1992" was the 1994 Phi Beta Kappa poem of the Nu Chapter of Massachusetts, University of Massachusetts—Amherst. "A History of Paisley" received a Pushcart Prize and appeared in *The Pushcart Prize XX*. It also appeared in the Summer 1996 issue of *Asian Art & Culture* (Oxford University Press in association with the Arthur M. Sackler Gallery, Smithsonian Institution).

I must thank various individuals for some unusual as well as the usual reasons: Rukun Advani, Anjum Ahmed, John Balaban, Tess Gallagher, Daniel Hall, Rafique Kathwari, Anthony Lacavaro, Jeanne McCulloch, Christopher Merrill, Lawrence Needham, Elise Paschen, Carol Houck Smith, Sara Suleri Goodyear, James Tate, Fred Wagner, and Dara Wier.

Contents

The Hour draws nigh and
the moon is rent asunder.

—THE KORAN
SURAH 54.1

The Blessèd Word: A Prologue

We shall meet again, in Petersburg
—OSIP MANDELSTAM

I

From an untitled poem, that opening line announces heartbreak as its craft: a promise like that already holds its own breaking: "We shall meet again, in Petersburg / as though we had buried the sun there."

From Kashmir, that Vale where the Titans sought refuge, where, just before Saturn began to speak to Thea, "There was a listening fear in her regard / As if calamity had but begun," from there: "When you leave home in the morning, you never know if you'll return." "We shall meet again, in Srinagar," I want to answer Irfan. But such a promise? I make it in Mandelstam's velvet dark, in the black velvet Void.

II

Let me cry out in that void, say it as I can. I write on that void: Kashmir, Kaschmir, Cashmere, Qashmir, Cashmir, Cashmire, Kashmere, Cachemire, Cushmeer, Cachmiere, Cašmir. Or *Cauchemar* in a sea of stories? Or: Kacmir, Kaschemir, Kasmere, Kachmire, Kasmir. Kerseymere?

He reinvents Petersburg (I, Srinagar), an imaginary homeland, filling it, closing it, shutting himself (myself) in it. For there is the blessèd word with no meaning, there are flowers that will never die, roses that will never fall, a night in which Mandelstam is not afraid and needs no pass. The blessèd women are still singing.

A patrol is stationed on the bridge and a car hoots like a cuckoo.

Maybe the ages will die away and the loved hands of blesséd women will brush the light ashes together?

III

And the night's sun there in Srinagar? Guns shoot stars into the sky, the storm of constellations night after night, the infinite that rages on. It was Id-uz-Zuha: a record of God's inability, for even He must melt sometimes, to let Ishmael be executed by the hand of his father. Srinagar was under curfew. The identity pass may or may not have helped in the crackdown. Son after son— never to return from the night of torture—was taken away.

IV

And will the blesséd women rub the ashes together? Each fall they gather *chinar* leaves, singing what the hills have reechoed for four hundred years, the songs of Habba Khatun, the peasant girl who became the queen. When her husband was exiled from the Valley by the Moghul king Akbar, she went among the people with her sorrow. Her grief, alive to this day, in her own roused the people into frenzied opposition to Moghul rule. And since then Kashmir has never been free.

And will the blesséd women rub the ashes together? Each fall, they sing her songs. They create their rustic fuel for winter: they set fire to the leaves, sprinkle water on them as they burn, and transform them into fragile coals.

But the reports are true, and without song: mass rapes in the villages, towns left in cinders, neighborhoods torched. "Power is hideous / like a barber's hands." The rubble of downtown Srinagar stares at me from the *Times*.

Maybe the ages will die away—we will pray in Mandelstam's night—and the loved hands of blesséd women will brush the light ashes together?

V

And that blesséd word with no meaning—who will utter it? What is it? Will the women pronounce it, as if scripturing the air, for the first time? Or the last?

Srinagar hunches like a wild cat: lonely sentries, wretched in bunkers at the city's bridges, far from their homes in the plains, licensed to kill . . . while the Jhelum flows under them, sometimes with a dismembered body. On Zero Bridge the jeeps rush by. The candles go out as travelers, unable to light up the velvet Void.

What is the blesséd word? Mandelstam gives no clue. One day the Kashmiris will pronounce that word truly for the first time.

(for Irfan Hasan)

I

Solitudinum faciunt et pacem appellant.

—TACITUS
(SPEAKING THROUGH A
BRITISH CHIEFTAIN REGARD-
ING PAX ROMANA)

Farewell

At a certain point I lost track of you.

They make a desolation and call it peace.

When you left even the stones were buried:

The defenceless would have no weapons.

When the ibex rubs itself against the rocks, who collects
    its fallen fleece from the slopes?

O Weaver whose seams perfectly vanished, who weighs the
    hairs on the jeweler's balance?

They make a desolation and call it peace.

Who is the guardian tonight of the Gates of Paradise?

My memory is again in the way of your history.

Army convoys all night like desert caravans:

In the smoking oil of dimmed headlights, time dissolved—all
    winter—its crushed fennel.

We can't ask them: *Are you done with the world?*

In the lake the arms of temples and mosques are locked
in each other's reflections.

Have you soaked saffron to pour on them when they are
found like this centuries later in this country
I have stitched to your shadow?

In this country we step out with doors in our arms.

Children run out with windows in their arms.

You drag it behind you in lit corridors.

If the switch is pulled you will be torn from everything.

At a certain point I lost track of you.

You needed me. You needed to perfect me:

In your absence you polished me into the Enemy.

Your history gets in the way of my memory.

I am everything you lost. You can't forgive me.

I am everything you lost. Your perfect enemy.

Your memory gets in the way of my memory:

I am being rowed through Paradise on a river of Hell:
Exquisite ghost, it is night.

The paddle is a heart; it breaks the porcelain waves:

It is still night. The paddle is a lotus:

I am rowed—as it withers—toward the breeze which is soft as
    if it had pity on me.

If only somehow you could have been mine, what wouldn't
    have happened in this world?

I'm everything you lost. You won't forgive me.

My memory keeps getting in the way of your history.

There is nothing to forgive. You won't forgive me.

I hid my pain even from myself; I revealed my pain only to
    myself.

There is everything to forgive. You can't forgive me.

If only somehow you could have been mine,

what would not have been possible in the world?

(for Patricia O'Neill)

I See Kashmir from New Delhi at Midnight

1

One must wear jeweled ice in dry plains
to will the distant mountains to glass.
The city from where no news can come
is now so visible in its curfewed night
that the worst is precise:

                              From Zero Bridge
a shadow chased by searchlights is running
away to find its body. On the edge
of the Cantonment, where Gupkar Road ends,
it shrinks almost into nothing, is

nothing by Interrogation gates
so it can slip, unseen, into the cells:
Drippings from a suspended burning tire
are falling on the back of a prisoner,
the naked boy screaming, "I know nothing."

2

The shadow slips out, beckons *Console Me*,
and somehow there, across five hundred miles,
I'm sheened in moonlight, in emptied Srinagar,
but without any assurance for him.

On Residency Road, by Mir Pan House,
unheard we speak: "I know those words by heart
(you once said them by chance): In autumn
when the wind blows sheer ice, the *chinar* leaves
fall in clusters—

                    one by one, otherwise."
"Rizwan, it's you, Rizwan, it's you," I cry out
as he steps closer, the sleeves of his *phiren* torn.
"Each night put Kashmir in your dreams," he says,
then touches me, his hands crusted with snow,
whispers, "I have been cold a long, long time."

      3

"Don't tell my father I have died," he says,
and I follow him through blood on the road
and hundreds of pairs of shoes the mourners
left behind, as they ran from the funeral,
victims of the firing. From windows we hear
grieving mothers, and snow begins to fall
on us, like ash. Black on edges of flames,
it cannot extinguish the neighborhoods,
the homes set ablaze by midnight soldiers.
Kashmir is burning:

                    By that dazzling light
we see men removing statues from temples.
We beg them, "Who will protect us if you leave?"
They don't answer, they just disappear
on the road to the plains, clutching the gods.

4

I won't tell your father you have died, Rizwan,
but where has your shadow fallen, like cloth
on the tomb of which saint, or the body
of which unburied boy in the mountains,
bullet-torn, like you, his blood sheer rubies
on Himalayan snow?

                    I've tied a knot
with green thread at Shah Hamdan, to be
untied only when the atrocities
are stunned by your jeweled return, but no news
escapes the curfew, nothing of your shadow,
and I'm back, five hundred miles, taking off
my ice, the mountains granite again as I see
men coming from those Abodes of Snow
with gods asleep like children in their arms.

                    (for Molvi Abdul Hai)

The Last Saffron

*Next to saffron cultivation in interest come the floating gardens
of the Dal Lake that can be towed from place to place.*

1

I will die, in autumn, in Kashmir,
and the shadowed routine of each vein
will almost be news, the blood censored,
for the *Saffron Sun* and the *Times of Rain*

will be sold in black, then destroyed,
invisibly at Zero Taxi Stand.
There will be men nailing tabloids
to the fence of Grindlay's Bank,

I will look for any sign of blood
in captions under the photos of boys,
those who by inches—after the April flood—
were killed in fluted waters, each voice

torn from its throat as the Jhelum
receded to their accounts and found cash
sealed in the bank's reflection.
I will open the waves, draw each hushed

balance, ready to pay, by any means,
whatever the drivers ask. The one
called *Eyes of Maple Green*
will promise, "I'll take you anywhere, even

in curfew hours," and give me a bouquet—
"There's a ban on wreaths!"

2

I will die that day in late October, it will be long ago:

He will take me to Pampore where I'll gather flowers and run
back to the taxi, stamens—How many thousands?—crushed to
red varnish in my hands: I'll shout: "Saffron, my payment!" And
he'll break the limits, chase each rumor of me. "No one's seen
Shahid," we'll hear again and again, in every tea house from
Nishat to Naseem. He will stop by the Shalimar *ghats*, and we'll
descend the steps to the water. He'll sever some land—two
yards—from the shore, I, his last passenger. Suddenly he'll age,
his voice will break, his gaze green water, washing me: "It won't
grow again, this gold from the burned fields of Pampore." And
he will row the freed earth past the Security zones, so my blood
is news in the *Saffron Sun* setting on the waves.

3

        Yes, I remember it,
the day I'll die, I broadcast the crimson,

so long ago of that sky, its spread air,
its rushing dyes, and a piece of earth

bleeding, apart from the shore, as we went
on the day I'll die, past the guards, and he,

keeper of the world's last saffron, rowed me
on an island the size of a grave. On

two yards he rowed me into the sunset,
past all pain. On everyone's lips was news

of my death but only that beloved couplet,
broken, on his:

"If there is a paradise on earth,
It is this, it is this, it is this."

               (for Vidur Wazir)

I Dream I Am the Only Passenger on Flight 423 to Srinagar,

and when we—as if from ashes—ascend
into the cold where the heart must defend

its wings of terror and even pity
and below us the haze of New Delhi

grays, *In your eyes I look for my wounds' deep sea.*
But five hundred years waved with history?

It is to song that one must turn for flight.
But with what measure will I shed sunlight

on pain? *In your eyes*—Was her sari turquoise?—
I look for the deep sea . . . That is her voice—

Begum Akhtar's. "You were the last, we know,
to see her in Delhi, Desperado

in search of catastrophe." Heartbreak of perfume
is mine again. The pilot turns up the volume:

Attar—of jasmine? What was it she wore
that late morning in October '74

when we were driven (it was the sunniest
day) from Connaught Place to Palam Airport? She pressed

a note—Rs. 100—into my palm:
"Take it or, on my life, I will perish."

They announced DEPARTURE. I touched her arm.
Her sari *was* turquoise! She turned to vanish,

but then turned to wave. (*My silk is stained,
How will I face my Lord?* she'd set in Pain—

her chosen raga that July in Srinagar.)
A week later: GHAZAL QUEEN BEGUM AKHTAR

IS DEAD. She had claimed her right-to-die:
She had sung "Everyone Will Be Here But I"

those days in every city and trebled that nocturne
desperately—with love—to aubade.

Drunk one night, she had wept, "Shahid, I yearn
to die." What was her encore there in Ahmedabad—

the last song of her last concert? In the middle
of the night they took her to Intensive Care.

Alone, in words whirled in the hospital,
her heart had set—forever solitaire.

The hostess pours tea, hands me the *Statesman*:
31 October 1974?
BEGUM AKHTAR IS DEAD: under the headline:

her picture: she smiles: she lights a Capstan.
Sharp in flame, her face dissolves in smoke.
                                        IT'S WAR:
It's 1994: ARMY LAYS SIEGE TO SHRINE,

and on the intercom her ghazal fades . . .
The pilot's voice brings the news alive. Below us,
the mountains quicken cremation's shades,

and up here the sky rainbows itself. Was it thus
that Lal Ded—robed in the brilliant green
of Paradise—rose from her ashes, fabulous

with *My body blazed?* Could she have then foreseen
the tongue survive its borrowed alphabets?
She blessed her true heir: Sheikh Noor-ud-Din.

He still speaks through five centuries of poets.
I hear his voice: "Fire moves on its quick knees—
through Chrar-e-Sharif—toward my shrine. Know it's

time to return there—before ash filigrees
roses carved in the wood of weeping trees."

I ask, "Will the dry branches, Prophesier,
blaze again with blossom? *On its pyre*

the phoenix is dear to destiny." We begin
our descent. "All threads must be untied

before springtime. Ask all—Muslim and Brahmin—
if their wish came true?" He appears beside

me, cloaked in black: "Alas! Death has bent my back.
It is too late for threads at Chrar-e-Sharif."

The landing gear roars, we touch the ashen tarmac.
He holds my hand speechless to tell me if

those smashed golds flying past those petrified
reds are autumn's last crimsoned spillage

rushing with wings down the mountainside
or flames clinging to a torched village.

(for Krishna Misri)

"Some Vision of the World Cashmere"

If I could bribe them by a Rose
I'd bring them every flower that grows
From Amherst to Cashmere!

—EMILY DICKINSON

I

But the phone rings, here in Amherst: "Your grandmother is dying. Our village is across the bridge over the flood channel, the bridge named for Mahjoor."

"There's no such village!"

"She had a terrible fall. There is curfew everywhere. We have no way to bring her back. There is panic on the roads. Our neighbors have died."

There never was such a village . . .

"We are your relatives from her mother's mother's side. You've heard of us! We once were traders and sold silk carpets to princes in Calcutta, but now we are poor and you have no reason to know us."

II

I put the phone down in Srinagar and run into the sunlight toward her cottage in our garden. Except for her dressing table mirror which Sikander, so long dead, is polishing, the army has occupied her house, made it their dingy office, dust everywhere, on old phones, on damp files, on broken desks. In her drawing room a clerk types. The colonel, dictating, turns around. My lost friend Vir! Srinagar is his city, too, he wouldn't have ordered its burning. It's not him. Someone else with a smile just as kind, the face of a man who in dreams saves nations. Or razes cities.

"My grandmother is ill. Please send someone with me. Please, someone with me in one of your jeeps to the village."

III

In her room the sun shines on her father—a painting from which he stares, unblinded, at even today's sunlight.

Just then through the back gate some villagers and her dead brother are bringing her slowly through the poplars, by the roses. I run out: *Thank God you're alive!* She is telling her brother, *Be grateful you died before these atrocities. My small home a dark office! How will I welcome you?*

IV

The mirrors have grieved in her absence. They run to greet her at the door. It is her home again! Sikander has turned on the radio: a song of Mahjoor's, in Raj Begum's voice: "The whole universe is worth nothing more than your shadow." And I'm holding her hand in that sun which is shining on all the summers of my childhood, shining on a teardrop in which windows are opening, amplifying her voice, and she is telling me, *God is merciful, God is compassionate.*

"Lo, A Tint Cashmere! /
Lo, A Rose!"

—EMILY DICKINSON

I

There was another summer: we were listening to Radio Kashmir: the bell announced that second of the sunset: we broke our fasts: then a song:

Now again, summer: a summer of the last Yes: we are in the verandah, listening: on Radio Kashmir, a song: "What can one surrender but the heart? / I yield my remaining years to you."

She is still somehow holding the world together: she is naming the roses:

God loves me, no, He's in love with me, He is a jealous God, He can't bear my love for you, and you are my favorite grandchild. My poet grandson, why don't you write of love?

She is reliving with me her dream within a dream within a dream: the mirrors compete for her reflection: I see her with endless arms: I see her without beginning middle or end: it is the last summer of peace: it is the last summer of the last Yes: we are still somehow holding the world together: we are naming the roses: she lifts her lines of Fate and Life and Heart and Mind and presses them, burning, into my palms. And then Lo, in her empty hands, I see a Rose!

II

"So there is Revolution each day in the heart, / Let Sorrow's resplendent autocracy remain."

Now again, summer: a summer of the last Yes: we are in the verandah, listening:

"So there is Revolution each day in the heart" . . . That must be Faiz? I stopped praying once. Once. "The earth cried out as I bent my forehead to the ground: / You've crushed me forever with the weight of your faith."

III

She is still somehow holding the world together: she is naming the roses:

Listen, some winters ago I was with Nasir in Delhi. Word came from America: Nuzhat was dying. And I was left alone. Only his alcoholic servant and I! I fell ill, I couldn't walk. The servant said: This is God's will! A nurse from the nearby dispensary gave me an injection. I fell into some half-dream, half-sleep, in fever—I don't know how long. I see three women, two I recognized, but who is the third? I must be dead and they've come to bury me. No, they will persuade me to live! In a nursing home, they gave me a beautiful room. Outside my window the garden is full of flowers. And I am dead and this is Paradise and what a beautiful place God has given me.

IV

Her dream within a dream within a dream:

Then through the window I see my father and my husband. They were so young. They are coming toward me, and I wake up in the dream and tell the doctor, Don't prolong my agony, don't you see, my husband and father have come to call me. The doctor is telling those women, She's not cooperating. No, I will take the medicines, I don't want to die. But I see my husband and my father—O how long they have been dead! They are so young! They are in the garden and I am dead and I must have done good for God to grant me this world of flowers.

Ghazal

Pale hands I loved beside the Shalimar
—LAURENCE HOPE

Where are you now? Who lies beneath your spell tonight
before you agonize him in farewell tonight?

Pale hands that once loved me beside the Shalimar:
Whom else from rapture's road will you expel tonight?

Those "Fabrics of Cashmere—" "to make Me beautiful—"
"Trinket"—to gem—"Me to adorn—How—tell"—tonight?

I beg for haven: Prisons, let open your gates—
A refugee from Belief seeks a cell tonight.

Executioners near the woman at the window.
Damn you, Elijah, I'll bless Jezebel tonight.

Lord, cried out the idols, *Don't let us be broken;
Only we can convert the infidel tonight.*

Has God's vintage loneliness turned to vinegar?
He's poured rust into the Sacred Well tonight.

In the heart's veined temple all statues have been smashed.
No priest in saffron's left to toll its knell tonight.

He's freed some fire from ice, in pity for Heaven;
he's left open—for God—the doors of Hell tonight.

And I, Shahid, only am escaped to tell thee—
God sobs in my arms. Call me Ishmael tonight.

II

No idea, even an idea as close to many Russians as the indivisibility of Russia, can justify a war against a whole people.

—ELENA BONNER
OPEN LETTER TO YELTSIN
ON CHECHNYA

No human being or group of people has the right to pass a death sentence on a city.

—CHARLES SIMIC

Dear Shahid,

I am writing to you from your far-off country. Far even from us who live here. Where you no longer are. Everyone carries his address in his pocket so that at least his body will reach home.

Rumors break on their way to us in the city. But word still reaches us from border towns: Men are forced to stand barefoot in snow waters all night. The women are alone inside. Soldiers smash radios and televisions. With bare hands they tear our houses to pieces.

You must have heard Rizwan was killed. Rizwan: Guardian of the Gates of Paradise. Only eighteen years old. Yesterday at Hideout Café (everyone there asks about you), a doctor—who had just treated a sixteen-year-old boy released from an interrogation center—said: *I want to ask the fortune-tellers: Did anything in his line of Fate reveal that the webs of his hands would be cut with a knife?*

This letter, *insh'Allah*, will reach you for my brother goes south tomorrow where he shall post it. Here one can't even manage postage stamps. Today I went to the post office. Across the river. Bags and bags—hundreds of canvas bags—all undelivered mail. By chance I looked down and there on the floor I saw this letter addressed to you. So I am enclosing it. I hope it's from someone you are longing for news of.

Things here are as usual though we always talk about you. Will you come soon? Waiting for you is like waiting for spring. We are waiting for the almond blossoms. And, if God wills, O! those days of peace when we all were in love and the rain was in our hands wherever we went.

A Pastoral

on the wall the dense ivy of executions
—ZBIGNIEW HERBERT

We shall meet again, in Srinagar,
by the gates of the Villa of Peace,
our hands blossoming into fists
till the soldiers return the keys
and disappear. Again we'll enter
our last world, the first that vanished

in our absence from the broken city.
We'll tear our shirts for tourniquets
and bind the open thorns, warm the ivy
into roses. Quick, by the pomegranate—
the bird will say—Humankind can bear
everything. No need to stop the ear

to stories rumored in branches: We'll hear
our gardener's voice, the way we did
as children, clear under trees he'd planted:
"It's true, my death, at the mosque entrance,
in the massacre, when the Call to Prayer
opened the floodgates"—Quick, follow the silence—

"and dawn rushed into everyone's eyes."
Will we follow the horned lark, pry
open the back gate into the poplar groves,
go past the search post into the cemetery,
the dust still uneasy on hurried graves
with no names, like all new ones in the city?

"It's true" (we'll hear our gardener
again). "That bird is silent all winter.
Its voice returns in spring, a plaintive cry.
That's when it saw the mountain falcon
rip open, in mid-air, the blue magpie,
then carry it, limp from the talons."

Pluck the blood: My words will echo thus
at sunset, by the ivy, but to what purpose?
In the drawer of the cedar stand,
white in the verandah, we'll find letters:
When the post offices died, the mailman
knew we'd return to answer them. Better

if he'd let them speed to death,
blacked out by Autumn's Press Trust—
not like this, taking away our breath,
holding it with love's anonymous
scripts: "See how your world has cracked.
Why aren't you here? Where are you? Come back.

Is history deaf there, across the oceans?"
Quick, the bird will say. And we'll try
the keys, with the first one open the door
into the drawing room. Mirror after mirror,
textiled by dust, will blind us to our return
as we light oil lamps. The glass map of our country,

still on the wall, will tear us to lace—
We'll go past our ancestors, up the staircase,
holding their wills against our hearts. Their wish
was we return—forever!—and inherit (Quick, the bird
will say) that to which we belong, not like this—
to get news of our death after the world's.

(for Suvir Kaul)

Return to Harmony 3

Two summers? Epochs, then, of ice.

But the air is the same muslin, beaten by the sky on Nanga Parbat, then pressed on the rocks of the nearer peaks.

I run down the ramp.

On the tarmac, I eavesdrop on Operation Tiger: Troops will burn down the garden and let the haven remain.

This is home—the haven a cage surrounded by ash—the fate of Paradise.

Through streets strewn with broken bricks and interrupted by paramilitaries, Irfan drives me straight to the Harmonies ("3" for my father—the youngest brother!), three houses built in a pastoral, that walled acreage of Harmonies where no one but my mother was poor.

A bunker has put the house under a spell. Shadowed eyes watch me open the gate, like a trespasser.

Has the gardener fled?

The Annexe of the Harmonies is locked—my grandmother's cottage—where her sons offered themselves to her as bouquets of mirrors. There was nothing else to reflect.

Under the windows the roses have choked in their beds. Was the gardener killed?

And the postman?

In the drawer of the cedar stand peeling in the verandah, a pile of damp letters—one to my father to attend a meeting the previous autumn, another an invitation to a wedding.

My first key opens the door. I break into quiet. The lights work.

The Koran still protects the house, lying strangely wrapped in a *jamawar* shawl where my mother had left it on the walnut table by the fireplace. Above, *If God is with you, Victory is near!*—the framed calligraphy ruthless behind cobwebs.

I pick up the dead phone, its number exiled from its instrument, a refugee among forlorn numbers in some angry office on Exchange Road.

But the receiver has caught a transmission: Rafi's song from a film about war: *Slowly, I so slowly, kept on walking, / and then was severed forever from her.* THIS IS ALL INDIA RADIO, AMRITSAR. I hang up.

Upstairs, the window, too, is a mirror; if I jump through it I will fall into my arms.

The mountains return my stare, untouched by blood.

On my shelf, by Ritsos and Rilke and Cavafy and Lorca and Iqbal and Amichai and Paz, my parents are beautiful in their wedding brocades, so startlingly young!

And there in black and white my mother, eighteen years old, a year before she came a bride to these Harmonies, so unforgivingly poor and so unforgivingly beautiful that the house begins to shake in my arms, and when the unarmed world is still again, with pity, it is the house that is holding me in its arms and the cry coming faded from its empty rooms is my cry.

The Country Without a Post Office

. . . *letters sent*
To dearest him that lives alas! away.
—GERARD MANLEY HOPKINS

1

Again I've returned to this country
where a minaret has been entombed.
Someone soaks the wicks of clay lamps
in mustard oil, each night climbs its steps
to read messages scratched on planets.
His fingerprints cancel blank stamps
in that archive for letters with doomed
addresses, each house buried or empty.

Empty? Because so many fled, ran away,
and became refugees there, in the plains,
where they must now will a final dewfall
to turn the mountains to glass. They'll see
us through them—see us frantically bury
houses to save them from fire that, like a wall,
caves in. The soldiers light it, hone the flames,
burn our world to sudden papier-mâché

inlaid with gold, then ash. When the muezzin
died, the city was robbed of every Call.
The houses were swept about like leaves
for burning. Now every night we bury
our houses—and theirs, the ones left empty.
We are faithful. On their doors we hang wreaths.
More faithful each night fire again is a wall
and we look for the dark as it caves in.

2

"We're inside the fire, looking for the dark,"
one card lying on the street says. "I want
to be he who pours blood. To soak your hands.
Or I'll leave mine in the cold till the rain
is ink, and my fingers, at the edge of pain,
are seals all night to cancel the stamps."
The mad guide! The lost speak like this. They haunt
a country when it is ash. Phantom heart,

pray he's alive. I have returned in rain
to find him, to learn why he never wrote.
I've brought cash, a currency of paisleys
to buy the new stamps, rare already, blank,
no nation named on them. Without a lamp
I look for him in houses buried, empty—
He may be alive, opening doors of smoke,
breathing in the dark his ash-refrain:

"Everything is finished, nothing remains."
I must force silence to be a mirror
to see his voice again for directions.
Fire runs in waves. Should I cross that river?
Each post office is boarded up. Who will deliver
parchment cut in paisleys, my news to prisons?
Only silence can now trace my letters
to him. Or in a dead office the dark panes.

3

"The entire map of the lost will be candled.
I'm keeper of the minaret since the muezzin died.
Come soon, I'm alive. There's almost a paisley
against the light, sometimes white, then black.
The glutinous wash is wet on its back
as it blossoms into autumn's final country—
Buy it, I issue it only once, at night.
Come before I'm killed, my voice canceled."

In this dark rain, be faithful, Phantom heart,
this is your pain. Feel it. You must feel it.
"Nothing will remain, everything's finished,"
I see his voice again: "This is a shrine
of words. You'll find your letters to me. And mine
to you. Come soon and tear open these vanished
envelopes." And I reach the minaret:
I'm inside the fire. I have found the dark.

This is your pain. You must feel it. Feel it,
Heart, be faithful to his mad refrain—
For he soaked the wicks of clay lamps,
lit them each night as he climbed these steps
to read messages scratched on planets.
His hands were seals to cancel the stamps.
This is an archive. I've found the remains
of his voice, that map of longings with no limit.

4

I read them, letters of lovers, the mad ones,
and mine to him from whom no answers came.
I light lamps, send my answers, Calls to Prayer
to deaf worlds across continents. And my lament
is cries countless, cries like dead letters sent
to this world whose end was near, always near.
My words go out in huge packages of rain,
go there, to addresses, across the oceans.

It's raining as I write this. I have no prayer.
It's just a shout, held in, It's Us! It's Us!
whose letters are cries that break like bodies
in prisons. Now each night in the minaret
I guide myself up the steps. Mad silhouette,
I throw paisleys to clouds. The lost are like this:
They bribe the air for dawn, this their dark purpose.
But there's no sun here. There is no sun here.

Then be pitiless you whom I could not save—
Send your cries to me, if only in this way:
I've found a prisoner's letters to a lover—
One begins: "These words may never reach you."
Another ends: "The skin dissolves in dew
without your touch." And I want to answer:
I want to live forever. What else can I say?
It rains as I write this. Mad heart, be brave.

(for James Merrill)

The Floating Post Office

The post boat was like a gondola
that called at each houseboat. It
carried a clerk, weighing scales,
and a bell to announce arrivals.

Has he been kept from us? Portents
of rain, rumors, ambushed letters . . .
Curtained palanquin, fetch our word,
bring us word: Who has died? Who'll live?
Has the order gone out to close
the waterways . . . the one open road?

And then we saw the boat being rowed
through the fog of death, the sentence
passed on our city. It came close
to reveal smudged black-ink letters
which the postman—he *was* alive—
gave us, like signs, without a word,

and we took them, without a word.
From our deck we'd seen the hill road
bringing a jade rain, near-olive,
down from the temple, some penitent's
cymbaled prayer? He took our letters,
and held them, like a lover, close

to his heart. And the rain drew close.
Was there, we asked, a new password—
blood, blood shaken into letters,
cruel primitive script that would erode
our saffron link to the past? Tense
with autumn, the leaves, drenched olive,

fell on graveyards, crying "O live!"
What future would the rain disclose?
O Rain, abandon all pretense,
now drown the world, give us your word,
ring, sweet assassin of the road,
the temple bell! For if letters

come, I will answer those letters
and my year will be tense, alive
with love! The temple receives the road:
there, the rain has come to a close.
Here the waters rise; our each word
in the fog awaits a sentence:

His hand on the scales, he gives his word:
Our letters will be rowed through olive
canals, tense waters no one can close.

The Correspondent

I say "There's no way back to your country,"
I tell him he must never leave. He cites
the world: his schedule. I set up barricades:
the mountain routes are damp;
there, dead dervishes damascene
the dark. "I must leave now," his voice ablaze.
I take off—it's my last resort—my shadow.

And he walks—there's no electricity—
back into my dark, murmurs *Kashmir!*, lights
(to a soundtrack of exploding grenades)
a dim kerosene lamp.
"We must give back the hour its sheen,
or this spell will never end. . . . Quick," he says,
"I've just come—with videos—from Sarajevo."

His footage is priceless with sympathy,
close-ups in slow motion: from bombed sites
to the dissolve of mosques in colonnades.
Then, wheelchairs on a ramp,
burning. He fast-forwards: the scene:
the sun: a man in formal wear: he plays
on the sidewalk his unaccompanied cello,

the hour tuned, dusk-slowed, to Albinoni,
only the *Adagio* as funeral rites
before the stars dazzle, polished to blades
above a barbed-wire camp.
The cellist disappears. The screen
fills—first with soldiers, then the dead, their gaze
fractured white with subtitles. Whose echo

inhabits the night? The phone rings. I think he
will leave. I ask: "When will the satellites
transmit my songs, carry Kashmir, aubades
always for dawns to stamp
True! across seas?" The stars careen
down, the lamp dies. He hangs up. A haze
settles over us. He opens the window,

points to convoys in the mountains, army
trucks with dimmed lights. He wants exclusive rights
to this dream, its fused quartz of furtive shades.
He's been told to revamp
his stories, reincarnadine
their gloss. I light a candle. He'll erase
Bosnia, I feel. He will rewind to zero,

film from there a way back to his country,
bypassing graves that in blacks and whites
climb ever up the hills. The wax cascades
down the stand, silver clamp
to fasten this dream, end it unseen.
In the faltering light, he surveys
what's left. He zooms madly into my shadow.

III

A Fate's Brief Memoir

1

A Fate—ask the stars!—gives no interviews,
but Visitor, dark from that doomed planet,
you have climbed the pitiful thread—blue noose

by which your life hangs—so I will let
myself answer you. My sisters should shortly
be here . . . this will be a brief tête-à-tête.

What is [clever question!] *the Fates' destiny?*
Always these scissors, only these scissors,
and in the stars' light each of us lonely

with threads—trillions: Cleopatra's. Caesar's.
O pardon me thou bleeding piece of earth—
I am well-read, you see, not always daggers

drawn. But we know nothing of our own birth.
Suddenly we were here—call us orphans—
beautiful certainly, with ties not worth

our while, each strand recalled by oblivion.
What a scribble, these questions on your sheet:
Do you also spin the threads of nations?

2

Are you feminists? YOU must be an athlete
to have climbed so neatly all this way to us.
We too outwit Ways we cannot defeat—

through dashes—so imagine! To become conscious
thus in this island universe—no past—
born cold holding steel in our hands? Jesus!

I never swear, but . . . notice the thinness
of breaths about to break. We recycle
them wholly black till their cobwebs incandesce

into—see those sheets: our letterhead: no last
name, just: FATE FATE FATE and then for address
(cross it out!) ~~ETERNITY~~. *That* we've outclassed.

3

So cruel then that each star be our jewel
and no one to witness it. For ornament,
my sisters empty nebulas by the fistful—

soon they will be here. The skies are rent
by stillborn suns. So glad that we have met,
that you have come; for, yes, we do miss men . . .

O that way madness lies . . . sweet heaven, O let
me not be mad . . . for when, by reflex, we execute
Heaven's texts—hammered on the Guarded Tablet—

we again learn our weakness: we can't commute
a sentence. My sister's hands—the youngest one's—
shook when she let a nation go. She uproots

stars, plucks them wildly—Call it adolescence—
and with their edges scratches the sky's glass.
After such knowledge what forgiveness? What defence?

At once aristocrat and working class,
keeping threads from entangling was her rapture.
Why should I tell you this? You will leave, alas!

O Fool! I shall go mad. Trespasser,
I must speak a little more. Avatars—
but of what?—we didn't know this would entrap her,

our sister's fingerprints dense on the stars.
Our hands gnarled with cutting, were we so wrong,
institutionalized thus in coeternal hours?

Finally no one is ours. You then will belong
to no one, too—not even me, your executioner.
You of course have known this all along?

I hold your breath. Look, I slow my fingers.
Do you now see why we give no interviews?
When you leave my hands will again be spiders.

What is this underlined? I hate *VALUES* . . .
I only prize a crisp prose: it sharpens
the dullest life. O, I've gone on. Well, spread this news:

PAST PRESENT FUTURE: not for us those prisons—
like the *Norns!* What a name! One thing we know:
we won't be compared with our Icelandic cousins;

they have no manner. Our ties are zero,
thinned with melting dew. We collapse all time—
the privilege of those with time; we go

on. Shall I give myself up (paradigm
from your world) for adoption? Who would refuse
me? *We will greet the time.* I ramble . . . I'm . . .

In this asylum one sings the madder blues.
But stay. Take care. Your hour will soon elapse.
My sisters—see them there—the stars bruise

their hands—rhinestones, really—well, let the chips
fall in whatever black hole. Galactic cluster,
what starry rubbish! Suddenly it's cold. What creeps

in spinning at this petty pace? A stiller
mankind breathes in caves, awaiting the Apocalypse.
No word yet looms of the Executioner.

What news may I give you of that Eclipse?
An implant already beats where the sun
has failed. Some hints then from my chilled lips:

4

There between planets the cobwebs thicken.
Depart now. Spiders look for my heart lest
I forget the final wreck of all that's human.

Farewell—and if thou livest or diest!
What poverty lets death exert its affluence?
The earth will receive you, poor honored guest,

and I minding my threadbare subsistence—
poor host who could offer you nothing. What brocades
spun from gasps I tear to polish our instruments . . .

threads searchlit, the universe dazzled, burnished blades . . .
Feel a new sun pounding—Dear Heart, this once!
See the famished sighs I'll lock into braids.

Don't forget this sight when by desolate chance
from your breath Belovéd! this evening fades.

(*for William Wadsworth*)

IV

At the Museum

But in 2500 B.C. Harappa,
who cast in bronze a servant girl?

No one keeps records
of soldiers and slaves.

The sculptor knew this,
polishing the ache

off her fingers stiff
from washing the walls

and scrubbing the floors,
from stirring the meat

and the crushed asafoetida
in the bitter gourd.

But I'm grateful she smiled
at the sculptor,

as she smiles at me
in bronze,

a child who had to play woman
to her lord

when the warm June rains
came to Harappa.

A History of Paisley

Their footsteps formed the paisley when Parvati, angry after a
quarrel, ran away from Shiva. He eventually caught up with her.
To commemorate their reunion, he carved the Jhelum river, as it
moves through the Vale of Kashmir, in the shape of paisley.

You who will find the dark fossils of paisleys
one afternoon on the peaks of Zabarvan—
Trader from an ancient market of the future,
alibi of chronology, that vain
collaborator of time—won't know that these

are her footprints from the day the world began
when land rushed, from the ocean, toward Kashmir.
And above the rising Himalayas? The air
chainstitched itself till the sky hung its bluest
tapestry. But already—as she ran

away—refugee from her Lord—the ruins
of the sea froze, in glaciers, cast in amber.
And there, in the valley below, the river
beguiled its banks into petrified longing:
(O see, it is still the day the world begins:

and the city rises, holding its remains,
its wooden beams already their own fire's prophets.)
And you, now touching sky, deaf to her anklets
still echoing in the valley, deaf to men
fleeing from soldiers into dead-end lanes

(Look! Their feet bleed; they leave footprints on the street
which will give up its fabric, at dusk, a carpet)—
you have found—you'll think—the first teardrop, gem
that was enticed for a Moghul diadem
into design. For you, blind to all defeat

up there in pure sunlight, your gauze of cloud thrown
off your shoulders over the Vale, do not hear
bullets drowning out the bells of her anklets.
This is her relic, but for you the first tear,
drop that you hold as you descend past flowstone,

past dried springs, on the first day of the world.
The street is rolled up, ready for southern ports.
Your ships wait there. What other cargo is yours?
What cables have you sent to tomorrow's bazaars?
What does that past await: the future unfurled

like flags? news from the last day of the world?
You descend quickly, to a garden-café:
At a table by a bed of tzigane
roses, three men are discussing, between
sips of tea, undiscovered routes on emerald

seas, ships with almonds, with shawls bound for Egypt.
It is dusk. The gauze is torn. A weaver kneels,
gathers falling threads. Soon he will stitch the air.
But what has made you turn? Do you hear her bells?
O, alibi of chronology, in what script

in your ledger will this narrative be lost?
In that café, where they discuss the promise
of the world, her cry returns from its abyss
where it hides, by the river. They don't hear it.
The city burns; the dusk has darkened to rust

by the roses. They don't see it. O Trader,
what news will you bring to your ancient market?
I saw her. A city was razed. In its debris
her bells echoed. I turned. They didn't see me
turn to see her—on the peaks—in rapid flight forever.

(for Anuradha Dingwaney)

A Footnote to History

Gypsies: . . . coming originally from India to Europe a thousand
years ago . . .

On the banks of the Indus,
just before

        it reaches
        the ocean,

and just before
the monsoons,

        they left
        me clutching

islands of farewells.

For ten centuries
they sent no word

though I often heard
through seashells

ships whispering for help.

I stuffed my pockets
with the sounds of wrecks.

I still can't decipher
scripts of storms

as I leaf through
the river's waves.

Half-torn by the wind,
their words reach

the shore, demanding
I memorize their

        ancient and recent
        journeys in

caravans ambushed by
forests on fire.

(for Bari Károly)

Son et Lumière at Shalimar Garden

Brahma's voice is torn water:

It runs down

       the slopes of Zabarvan
       and Kashmir is a lake

till a mountain to its west
is pierced with a trident

and the valley drained to reveal
the One Born of Water,

       now easily slain.

Who was that demon
of dessicated water?

No one knows
in the drying land

where a rattle of cones
is thatching

the roofs of kingdoms.

       We watch the wind.
       And unhealed,

the centuries pass:

Slaves plane the mountains
with roots they carried

in trunks from Isfahan:

Spotlights lash their backs
as Shalimar blooms into

the Moghuls' thirst for
terracing the seasons

                into symmetry.
                In the marble summer palace,

a nautch-girl pours wine
into the Emperor's glass,

splintering the future
into wars of succession,

the leaves scattered
as the wind blows

                an era into

another dynasty's bloody arms.

Ghazal

The only language of loss left in the world is Arabic—
These words were said to me in a language not Arabic.

Ancestors, you've left me a plot in the family graveyard—
Why must I look, in your eyes, for prayers in Arabic?

Majnoon, his clothes ripped, still weeps for Laila.
O, this is the madness of the desert, his crazy Arabic.

Who listens to Ishmael? Even now he cries out:
Abraham, throw away your knives, recite a psalm in Arabic.

From exile Mahmoud Darwish writes to the world:
You'll all pass between the fleeting words of Arabic.

The sky is stunned, it's become a ceiling of stone.
I tell you it must weep. So kneel, pray for rain in Arabic.

At an exhibition of miniatures, such delicate calligraphy:
Kashmiri paisleys tied into the golden hair of Arabic!

The Koran prophesied a fire of men and stones.
Well, it's all now come true, as it was said in the Arabic.

When Lorca died, they left the balconies open and saw:
his *qasidas* braided, on the horizon, into knots of Arabic.

Memory is no longer confused, it has a homeland—
Says Shammas: Territorialize each confusion in a graceful
    Arabic.

Where there were homes in Deir Yassein, you'll see dense
    forests—
That village was razed. There's no sign of Arabic.

I too, O Amichai, saw the dresses of beautiful women.
And everything else, just like you, in Death, Hebrew, and
    Arabic.

They ask me to tell them what *Shahid* means—
Listen: It means "The Belovéd" in Persian, "witness" in Arabic.

V

KENT. Is this the promis'd end?
EDGAR. Or image of that horror?

—*KING LEAR*

5.3.264–65

First Day of Spring

On this perfect day, perfect for forgetting God,
why are they—Hindu or Muslim, Gentile or Jew—
shouting again some godforsaken word of God?

The Angel, his wings flailing—no, burning—stood awed.
The Belovéd, dark with excessive bright, withdrew
and the day was not perfect for forgetting God.

On a face of stone it bends, the divining rod:
Not silver veins but tears: Niobe, whereunto
your slain children swaddled dark with the Names of God?

And now on earth, you and I, with longing so flawed
that: Angel forced to grow not wings but arms, why aren't you
holding me this day—perfect for forgetting God?

You spent these years on every street in Hell? How odd,
then, that I never saw you there, I who've loved you
against (*Hold me!*) against every word of God.

The rumor? It's again the reign of Nimrod.
Whoever you are, I depend on your message,
                                    but you—
        Angel I suspect no longer of God—
are still bringing me word from (*Could it be?*) from God.

Ghazal

adapted from Makhdoom Mohiuddin

Rumors of spring—they last from dawn till dusk—
All eyes decipher branches for blossoms.

Your legend now equals our thirst, Belovéd—
Your word has spread across broken nations.

Wherever each night I'm lost to myself,
they hear from me of Her—of Her alone.

Hope extinguished, now nothing else remains—
only nights of anguish, these ochre dawns.

The garden's eyes well up, the flower's heart beats
when we speak, just speak of O! Forever.

So it has, and forever it should last—
this rumor the Belovéd shares our pain.

Death Row

Someone else in this world has been mentioning you,

          gathering news, itemizing your lives
for a file you'll never see. He already knows

in which incarnation you won't find what you will
again lose in this one.

          He has traced your every
death. You need him now, but he's still asking about

you, with each question destroying your any chance
to find him. It was he

          whom you lost on your last
night alive in another life: he entered

your cell and you were reborn for that night as
anything he wanted: a woman when

          he asked for the love of women.

(for Hala Moddelmog)

The City of Daughters

God gave Noah the rainbow sign,
No more water, the fire next time!

(1990)

Who has flown in, pitiless, from the plains
with a crystal goblet in which—rum-dark!—
he sees the world? He drinks. And cold, the rains
come down. Now who will save Noah? The Ark

is set aflame, launched. And God? Here,
again, why I believe in Him: He put
his lips to my ear and said Nothing. Share,
then, my heart—anyone! Say farewell, cut

my heart loose, row its boat without me—
for I am leaving my world forever.
Say farewell, say farewell to the city
(O Sarajevo! O Srinagar!),

the Alexandria that is forever leaving.
I'm running toward a barbed-wire fence
and someone is running after me, shouting,
Take your name away, leave us in suspense:

whether you vanished? or survived? Garlands
replace the twisted wires, and I break free . . .
bullets fall, roses!, off me, and in my hands,
without a thread of blood, thorns bury

(1991)

their secrets. *No, Dream, remain with the waters.*
Troops pour into the City of Daughters
(his goblet is taken off the mantel shelf),
and I must row the heart all by myself,

I must row the heart (the world is rum-dark!),
I'll row it, but not by the rainbow's arc . . .
He sees the world; I'll row it by stardust,
I will sink it to find you, if I must,

for in this world below zero Fahrenheit
it's over, the Festival of Light:
From the shore through her hair blown black
a mother sees a fleet depart to sack

a city (a drum mimes the sunset wind:
In *Iphigenia* it's night and THE END . . .
Will you watch as her blood soaks the altar?
O too-late wind that did not save a daughter!) . . .

In the mosques of the city that is leaving
forever—suspended in lamps, with floating
wicks of oil—vessels flare, go out. The years
have come (Promise me, love, you will be there?),

(1993)

when I must spend my time on every street
in Hell. The Governor in his mansion rings
the crystal. It is refilled. The songs
in Sacredhair go out. An imperial fleet

of trucks—*No more water!*—enters the Square.
The shops are set afire. *Where are you, my love,*
in this world dyed orange—in one stroke mauve?
("God's secret: He put His lips to my ear

and didn't say a thing."—Jaime Sabines).
"Dear Shahid, they burned the Palladium."
There, the kiss each weekend at 7:00 P.M.
was enshrined, and we tried it, merciless

to ourselves—we pulled the kiss off the screen.
Then the Angel forced us to shut our eyes
when his wings red-darkened those epic skies:
In *A Tale of Two Cities* the guillotine

did not stop falling . . . *It is a far, far*
better thing that I do . . . But when the martyr
went ("Why wasn't he afraid to die?" cried Caesar),
smiling with each step to death, his lips ajar—

(1994)

targets for a kiss!—our eyes were open.
Now when bullets vine-scatter their petals
on our wall, what's left but the horizon
and a flame's bruised sulfur? After INTERVAL,

before walls burgeoned petal by petal,
a cigarette was alive in a finished world.
I again smell it, the struck matchstick. It's INTERVAL:
in a mansion rum-dark waters are swirled.

A cigarette was alive, and it's a finished world—
in autumn we planted its final embers.
The Ark rocked. The waters were swirled.
Troops poured into the City of Daughters.

No more water!—We again plant embers.
What's left to abolish in Lal Chowk?
Troops burn down the City of Daughters,
and a tree bursts into branches of smoke.

In his waters it's the end. In Lal Chowk,
what's left to abolish? There is no horizon.
From the tree we are tearing flowers of smoke,
no longer targets for a kiss, but our lips open.

* In South Asia, Interval is the term commonly used for Intermission.

Muharram in Srinagar, 1992

Death flies in, thin bureaucrat, from the plains—
a one-way passenger, again. The monsoon rains
smash their bangles, like widows, against the mountains.
Our hands disappear. He travels first-class, sipping cham-
    pagne.

One-way passengers again, the monsoon rains
break their hands. Will ours return, ever, to hold a bouquet?
He travels first-class. Our hands disappear. Sipping cham-
    pagne,
he goes through the morning schedule for Doomsday:

"Break their hands." Will ours return with guns, or a bouquet?
Ice hardens its fat near his heart. We're cut to the brains.
He memorizes, clause by clause, the contract for Doomsday.
We mourn the martyrs of Karbala, our skins torn with chains.

Ice hardens its fat in his heart, and we're cut to the brains.
Near the ramp colonels wait with garlands by a jeep.
(O mourners, Husain bleeds, tear your skins with chains!)
The plane lands. In the Vale the children are dead, or asleep.

He descends. The colonels salute. A captain starts the jeep.
The Mansion by the lake awaits him with roses. He's driven
through streets bereft of children: they are dead, not asleep.
O, when will our hands return, if only broken?

The Mansion is white, lit up with roses. He is driven
through streets in which blood flows like Husain's.
Our hands won't return to us, not even mutilated, when
Death comes—thin bureaucrat—from the plains.

*Muharram, the Muslim month of mourning, marks the martyrdom of
Husain (Prophet Mohammed's grandson) and his followers in the battle
of Karbala.

Hans Christian Ostro

*Even today there are no trains
into the Vale of Kashmir.*

And those defunct trains—Kashmir Mail,
Srinagar Express—took
pilgrims only till the last of the plains.
There, in blue-struck buses, they forsook
the monsoon. What iron could be forged to rail
like faith through mountains

star-sapphired, by dawn amethyst?
It's not a happy sound . . .
There is such pathos in the cry of trains:
Words breathed aloud but inward-bound.
Bruised by trust   O Heart bare amidst
fire   arms turquoise with veins

from love's smoke-mines   blesséd infidel
who wants your surrender?
I cannot protect you: these are my hands.
I'll wait by the deep-jade river;
you'll emerge from the mist of Jewel Tunnel:
O the peaks one commands—

A miracle!—from there . . . Will morning
suffice to dazzle blind
beggars to sight? *Whoso gives life to a soul*
shall be as if he had to all of mankind
given life. Or will your veins' hurt lightning—
the day streaked with charcoal—

betray you, beautiful stranger
sent to a lovelorn people
longing for God? Their river torn apart,
they've tied waves around their ankles,
mourning the train that save its passenger
will at night depart

for drowning towns. And draped in rain
of the last monsoon-storm,
a beggar, ears pressed to that metal cry,
will keep waiting on a ghost-platform,
holding back his tears, waving every train
Good-bye and Good-bye.

*Hans Christian Ostro was a twenty-seven-year-old Norwegian
hostage killed in Kashmir by the Al-Faran militants in August 1995.

A Villanelle

When the ruins dissolve like salt in water,
only then will they have destroyed everything.
Let your blood till then embellish the slaughter,

till dawn soaks up its inks, and "On their blotter
of fog the trees / Seem a botanical drawing."
Will the ruins dissolve like salt in water?

A woman combs—at noon—the ruins for her daughter.
Chechnya is gone. What roses will you bring—
plucked from shawls at dusk—to wreathe the slaughter?

Or are these words plucked from God that you've brought her,
this comfort: *They will not have destroyed everything*
till the ruins, too, are destroyed? Like salt in water,

what else besides God disappears at the altar?
O Kashmir, Armenia once vanished. Words are nothing,
just rumors—like roses—to embellish a slaughter:

these of a columnist: "The world will not stir";
these on the phone: "When you leave in the morning,
you never know if you'll return." Lost in water,
blood falters; then swirled to roses, it salts the slaughter.

After the August Wedding
in Lahore, Pakistan,

we all—Save the couple!—returned to pain,
some in Massachusetts, some in Kashmir
where, wet by turns, Order's dry campaign
had glued petals with bullets to each pane—
Sarajevo Roses! A gift to glass,
that city's name. What else breaks? A lover's pain!
But happiness? Must it, too, bring pain?
Question I may ask because of a night—
by ice-sculptures, all my words sylvanite
under one gaze that filled my glass with pain.
That thirst haunts as does the fevered dancing,
flames dying among orchids flown in from Sing-

apore! Sing then, not of the promising
but the Promised End. Of what final pain,
what image of that horror can I sing?
To be forgotten the most menacing!
Those "Houseboat Days in the Vale of Kashmir,"
for instance, in '29: Did they sing
just of love then, or was love witnessing
its departure for other thirsts—the glass
of Dal Lake ruffled half by "Satin Glass,"
that chandeliered boat barely focusing
on emptiness—last half of any night?
In Lahore the chanteuse crooned "Stop the Night"—

the groom's request—after the banquet. *Night,*
that Empress, is here, your bride. She will sing!
Her limbs break like chrysanthemums. O Night,
what hints have been passed in the sky tonight?
The stars so quiet, what galaxies of pain
leave them unable to prophesy this night?
With a rending encore, she closed the night.
There was, like this, long ago in Kashmir,
a moment—after a concert—outside Kashmir
Book Shop that left me stranded, by midnight,
in a hotel mirror. Would someone glass
me in—from what? Filled, I emptied my glass,

lured by a stranger's eyes into their glass.
There, nothing melted, as in Lahore's night:
Heat had brought sweat to the lip of my glass
but sculptures kept iced their aberrant glass.
To be forgotten my most menacing
image of the End—expelled from the glass
of someone's eyes as if no full-length glass
had held us, safe, from political storms? Pain,
then, becomes love's thirst—the ultimate pain
to lose a stranger! O, to have said, glass
in hand, "Where Thou art—that—is Home— / Cashmere—
or Calvary—the same"! In the Cašmir

and Poison and Brut air, my rare Cashmere
thrown off, the stranger knew my arms are glass,
that banished from Eden (on earth: Kashmir)
into the care of storms (it rains in Kashmir,
in Lahore, and here in Amherst tonight),
in each new body I would drown Kashmir.
A brigadier says, *The boys of Kashmir*
break so quickly, we make their bodies sing,
on the rack, till no song is left to sing.
"Butterflies pause / On their passage Cashmere—"
And happiness: must it only bring pain?
The century is ending. It is pain

from which love departs into all new pain:
Freedom's terrible thirst, flooding Kashmir,
is bringing love to its tormented glass.
Stranger, who will inherit the last night
of the past? Of what shall I not sing, and sing?

(for Shafaq Husain)

Notes

"THE BLESSÉD WORD":

The poem, throughout, alludes to W. S. Merwin's translation of
  Osip Mandelstam's poem.
Srinagar: The capital of Kashmir.
Id-uz-Zuha: One of Islam's most sacred days. To establish cen-
  trality for Ishmael (Father of the Arab nation), Muslims say it
  was he—not Isaac—whom God had asked Abraham to sacri-
  fice. The day is marked by festivity and the sacrifice of lambs
  and goats.
Habba Khatun: I am indebted to M. Mujeeb's *Indian Muslims*
  (George Allen & Unwin) for the historical details and for
  some of my phrasing.

"FAREWELL":

This poem at one—but only one—level is a plaintive love letter
  from a Kashmiri Muslim to a Kashmiri Pandit (the indigenous
  Hindus of Kashmir are called Pandits).
Saffron: The world's best saffron is believed to be grown in
  Kashmir and Iran (it takes the stigmata of seventy-five thou-
  sand flowers to make one pound of saffron). A paste made
  from it is used in various Hindu rituals. The *color* saffron is
  associated with Hindu traditions, green with Muslim culture.

Shah Hamdan (Sayyid'Ali Hamadani): One often refers to his shrine in Srinagar simply by his name. A Sufi saint, he paid three visits to Kashmir (1372, 1379, and 1383), and he was in effect responsible for the peaceful conversion of the Kashmiris to Islam. On his third visit he was accompanied by seven hundred scholars and clerics who estalished Sufi centers throughout Kashmir.

Green thread: It is customary for both Muslims and Hindus to go to Sufi shrines and make a wish there by tying a thread. Should the wish come true, one must return to untie it.

"I DREAM I AM THE ONLY PASSENGER ON FLIGHT 423 TO SRINAGAR,":

Begum Akhtar: One of the Indian subcontinent's greatest singers and certainly the greatest ghazal singer of all time. She died in 1974.

Lal Ded: Kashmiri mystic poet (1320?–1391?) whose verses are on almost every Kashmiri's lips. One of the many apocryphal legends associated with her has been recounted thus: "While wandering naked she spotted Hamadani [see the note for Shah Hamdan] and intuited his holiness. She cried out, 'I have seen a man!' and ran into a baker's shop, where she jumped into a blazing oven and was immediately consumed by the flames. When the saint came into the shop looking for her, she suddenly emerged from the oven dressed in an aura of the brilliant green of Paradise" (Daniel Halpern, ed. *Holy Fire*— HarperPerennial, p. 45).

Sheikh Noor-ud-Din (1377?–1438?): Patron saint of Kashmir who modernized the Kashmiri language. The destruction by fire of his shrine at Chrar-e-Sharif on 11 May 1995 was front-page news all over the world. John F. Burns reported in the *New York Times* (14 May 1995): "Despite Indian Army denials, the people who gathered to vent their fury insisted that it had been Indian troops, not Muslim militants besieged in the town, who set the fire—actually, two fires—that ran through the wondrous, toytown array of mostly wooden homes and bazaars and mosques that clung for centuries to the hillsides here, defying endless winters of bitter cold and summers of searing heat."

"On its pyre / the phoenix is dear to destiny": This is a free translation of a line of Sheikh Noor-ud-Din's, whose verses—marked by Sufi grace and wisdom—are also known to almost every Kashmiri.

"A FATE'S BRIEF MEMOIR":

This poem is spoken by Clotho, whom I imagine to be the oldest of the three Fates. Among her conscious allusions are to Shakespeare, T. S. Eliot, George Trakl, Apollinaire, W. H. Auden, and Thomas Mann.

Norns: Also three sisters like the Greek Fates, they are the Fates of Scandinavian mythology.

"Farewell—and if thou livest or diest!": The first sentence of the last paragraph of Thomas Mann's The Magic Mountain.

About the Author

Agha Shahid Ali, a Kashmiri-American, calls himself a multiple-exile. Director of the M.F.A. Program in Creative Writing at the University of Massachusetts—Amherst, he is a poet (his collections include *The Half-Inch Himalayas*, *A Walk Through the Yellow Pages*, and *A Nostalgist's Map of America*), translator (*The Rebel's Silhouette: Selected Poems by Faiz Ahmed Faiz*), and critic (*T. S. Eliot as Editor*). A recipient of fellowships from the Pennsylvania Council on the Arts, the Bread Loaf Writers' Conference, the Ingram-Merrill Foundation, the New York Foundation for the Arts, and the John Simon Guggenheim Memorial Foundation, he has previously taught at the University of Delhi, the Pennsylvania State University, the University of Arizona, and Hamilton College.